SHELL SHOCK
conchological curiosities

with 100 illustrations, 78 in color

PATRICK MAURIES

THAMES AND HUDSON

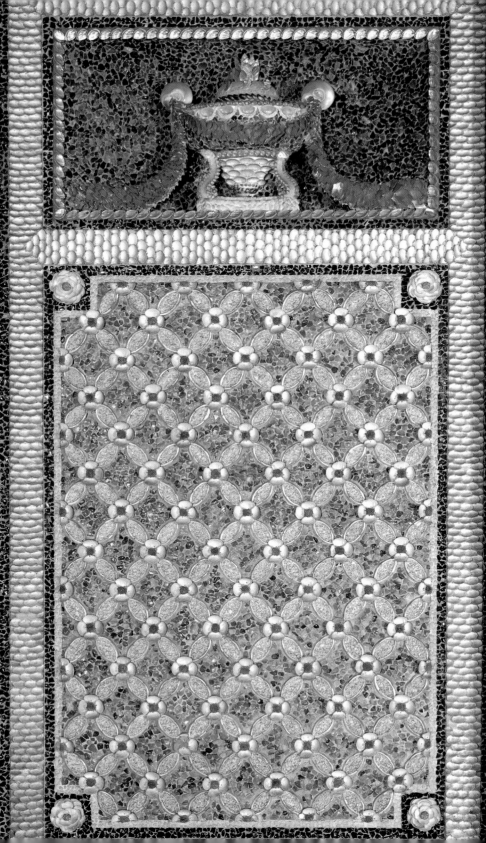

For Françoise de Nobèle

Page 1: *Anne Vallayer-Coster (1744–1818),* Sea Plume, *1769, oil on canvas, Musée du Louvre, Paris.*

Pages 2–3: *Plaster wall-light in the form of a shell, 1940s (39 cm high, 58 cm wide).*

Page 4: *White porcelain shell-shaped ornament, English popular art, early twentieth century.*

Page 5: *Winged dragon in chased and gilded bronze carrying a nautilus shell, French, mid-nineteenth century.*

Page 6: *Ballroom of Arturo Lopez-Willshaw's mansion in Neuilly, built in 1951 on the model of Marie-Antoinette's shell pavilion at Rambouillet (see page 64).*

Page 7: *Shell table in Louis XV style (73 cm high, 84 cm wide); Medici shell casket (26 cm high, 32 cm wide) and shell vase (64 cm high), made by Anne Vincent and Eric Chailloux for the Epoca gallery, Paris, 1993.*

Page 8: *Pierre Le-Tan,* The Strolling Hour *(20.5 x 19 cm),*

watercolour painted specially for this book.

Page 9: *Christian Lacroix, shell-shaped straw hat,* **haute couture** *collection, summer 1988.*

Page 12: *Arcimboldo-like face made up of rare shells on a lead support (44 x 34 cm), French, early eighteenth century.*

Page 14: *Jan van Kessell (Antwerp, 1626–1678),* **Still Life of Shells and Flowers,** *1654, oil on copper (31 x 43 cm), private collection.*

TRANSLATED FROM THE FRENCH *COQUILLAGES ET ROCAILLES* BY MICHAEL WOLFERS AND RONALD DAVIDSON-HOUSTON

The in-text drawings are by Pierre Le-Tan.

First published in the United States of America in 1994 by
Thames and Hudson Inc., 500 Fifth Avenue, New York, New York 10110

Library of Congress Catalog Card Number 93-61598

ISBN 0-500-01609-7

Printed and bound in France

CONTENTS

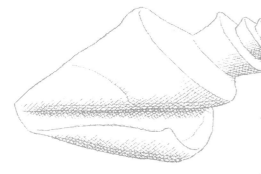

FOREWORD

An exhaustive treatment of the shell motif would take volumes and would have to incorporate much of the history of form. This brief offering intends rather to pick up the trail of a fantasy, to pursue the shifting interpretation of the motif through some of its history, through the lean and fat years, the low points and the high – things usually overlooked as insignificant, but really of abounding interest.

In short, this book considers the shell when it ceases to be a symbol and becomes a motif. The ancients are thought to have associated the shell with Aphrodite, whose statues stood within a shell-shaped niche. It is not entirely clear if this architectural form came directly from the myth of her sea-birth, or more simply from the material constraint of using brick. Paradoxically, the motif is also to be found associated with funerary rites and monuments.

The importance to the whole of the medieval Christian world of the pilgrimage to Santiago de Compostela is well known, along with the scallop symbol of St James. Religious painting from the early Italian Renaissance – from Fra Angelico to Filippo Lippi, from Piero della Francesca to Benozzo Gozzoli – is punctuated by Virgins in shell niches, echoes of images of the pagan Venus, whose form may be seen as embodying the architecture of a long-vanished ancient order.

Towards the end of the fifteenth century, Botticelli's *Birth of Venus* symbolizes the transition and the beginning of a desanctification. When the scallop frees itself from its purely architectural function to become, for instance, an infinitely variable component of a fountain, the story of the decorative motif is really beginning.

CHAPTER ONE THE SHAPELY SHELL

But why not one more turn?
Paul Valéry

The shell is a mass of paradoxes: small, yet monumental; rocklike, yet organic; geometrical, yet natural; Baroque in its exuberance, and yet exuding an unruffled calm. It unites the contradictory: a solid, rigid case to contain the most delicate of bodies; a lifelike corpse that survives long after the living creature has perished; a rough and wrinkled surface concealing the polished smoothness and milky glaze of mother-of-pearl; a treasure that is both plentiful and free.

The French poet and philosopher Paul Valéry, in a masterly turn of phrase, wrote that we can see in the shell 'the semblance of an invention'. The whole fascination of these natural objects seems tied to this conflict between the orderly and the accidental, the pure line and the raw material, immutable law and fantasy, the sudden imposition of a logic (or the appearance of it) on the confusion of reality. It is all to do with a bizarre artificiality that is at the same time completely natural.

The shell represents a whole that is more than the sum of its parts. It resonates with associations and with a host of different connotations. Its giddy gyration, frozen in motion, gives the shell the impression of unwinding endlessly on its spiral axis in perpetual, yet ultimately limited, development. This is the notion of progress so dear to Valéry, the image of the mental process, of the role of intelligence that aims 'to annihilate infinity and exterminate repetition'. It is a reflection of an object that rotates on itself in ceaseless self-revelation and in the exhilarating realization of an eventual fulfilment.

The shell invites protest at the seemingly impossible: it could surely not be anything but a human creation, yet it is nothing of the kind. This organic growth, with its mathematical asymmetry, has evolved from time immemorial, being shaped and reshaped through countless aeons to attain its final flawless form. It is the climax of a remote beginning and long-drawn-out process, a miraculous equilibrium of nature, like the graceful poise of a dancer arrested in mid-movement or the beauty of a flower at the peak of its perfection.

The phantom logic that shells suggest is almost certainly why throughout history they have inspired unusual features in decorative schemes. Compact packages, tiny fragments of the sublime, they became the instruments of an *ordo artificialis*, of a play of repetitive, rhapsodic motifs that, perversely, were of staggering precision. In the sixteenth and seventeenth centuries they found their way into cabinets of curiosities, symmetrically and artistically arranged. In the eighteenth century they were part of the illusionist patchwork of Grotesque décors, when every possible surface was covered with extraordinary coarsely textured designs. In the nineteenth century taste reached rock bottom with human and animal figures under bell-glass and folksy figurines. Here the shell seems to have become the chosen instrument of a relentless and methodical expansion, driven by a guiding spirit of proliferation that was both childlike and indulgent. (The twentieth century, by contrast, tends to include in its vocabulary of shapes the shell in its simplest state, purged of anomaly or ambiguity, as for example in the work of Serge Roche or Diego Giacometti.)

Too close a consideration of the natural object and its endless reverberations risks losing sight of the motif's past. The shell is the glowing heart of Grotesque taste, typifying a fantastical re-creation of a so-called 'Pompeiian' decoration, and rustic style, that extends throughout the history of modern aesthetics. Epitomizing asymmetry, the shell is essential to those 'low' cultures which, in opposition to the values of 'high' culture, are a regular stimulus to the history of form. As a free, dynamic form the shell, together with the scroll, directly inspires the Rocaille aesthetic, then the Rococo. Centuries later, the resurgence of this feeling for the Baroque as reinvented in the 1930s – a neglected chapter in the history of contemporary taste – shows all the vivacity and inexhaustible power of that resonance. The shell is both a creation of nature and an artificial object, steeped in history – a motif for all times and a reflection of the varying interpretation of each age.

Finally, the shell has its immediate correlations; it is known by many names – conch, clam, oyster, scallop, limpet, cowrie, murex, mussel – representing its complete, perfected shape. And then there is the vocabulary of fable – nautilus, buccinum, argonaut, tridacna – instruments of sea gods, attributes of mythological creatures bringing ancient voices from afar; barely perceptible whispers that carry us to wondrous shores belonging only to dream and to nostalgia; manifestations of sea and sun, of solidity and fluidity, whose paradoxical material is an inexhaustible source of wonder.

CHAPTER TWO THE CURIO CABINET

Modern Europe begins in the meticulously arranged settings created by an enlightened few, in which fragments of mummies jostle with fossilized ferns, armadillo carapaces with Red Indian chiefs' head-dresses, narwhal tusks with stuffed crocodiles, rock crystal with coral.

These were the cabinets of curiosities, collections of strange *naturalia* widely established in the sixteenth century. In France, Germany, England and Italy, collectors, scholars and lovers of the exotic believed that within the narrow confines of a room or a cabinet they could display the great diversity of the whole known world. Among them may be named Erasmus of Rotterdam, the Swiss Konrad von Gesner, the two John Tradescants, father and son, in Oxford, the Italian Ulisse Aldrovandi, and Father Claude Dumolinet in Paris. They hunted for symbols of the elsewhere – in time and in space – and the shell, a manifestation of unknown lands brought back from distant travels, had an essential place in these reflections of the world. Significantly, the first collections were assembled in the Low Countries, the centre of sea trade with the West and East Indies.

According to Julius von Schlosser, the curio cabinets owed their origin to the great medieval treasure houses that were statements of both political and religious sovereignty and which, more deeply still, expressed an underlying archaic phenomenon of projection ('external projection of the primitive concept of ownership as ornament'). The aim of the curio collectors was to possess a world that would all at once disclose its infinite variety, ceaselessly opening on new unknowns; to possess even a tiny particle of the extraordinary or inexplicable; to possess something not to be found in books, something quite unheard-of. If the assorted catalogues of the scientifically inclined tended to exhaust the multiplicity of objects, to round out a whole perspective, the collectors were more prone to rejoice in the exceptional, in accumulating rarities and in the infinite proliferation of wonders; they sought out the disjunction, contiguity, context and intensity of the unique.

Each object in general, and the shell in particular, had some kind of magical potency, some impossible aura; it was redolent of power and tacitly conferred on its owner a share in that power, the glamour of supremacy.

The arrangement of these unique items was vital: the cabinet was the place where an assortment of finds must be 'disposed in good order'; the 'good order' was a reflection of the rarity and incomparable quality of each object. The placing was purely for show: an assemblage of analogies and affinities, a play of symmetry and echo. Thus it was, quite naturally, that the fetishism of arrangement ran over into aesthetics and that natural history overflowed into the history of ornament.

The clearest sign of the significance of arrangement is the very make-up of the books and pictures that, from the second half of the seventeenth century onwards, recorded and celebrated the curio cabinets and their

Opposite: *Johann Georg Heinz (c. 1647–1713),* **Cabinet of Curiosities, 1666, Kunsthalle, Hamburg.** *Meticulously arranged on their shelves, the 'unique' curiosities of Heinz's collector, including shells and a skull, take on a hallucinatory, relief-like solidity with each fetishistic object standing out against an abstract background, bathed in a metaphysical light.*

Above: *Frans Francken the Younger (1581–1642),* **Cabinet of Curiosities, c. 1636, Kunsthistorisches Museum, Vienna.** *The funereal connotations of this world of riches and acquisitiveness also pervade Frans Francken's more anarchic* **Cabinet of Curiosities;** *but here there is no suggestion of any taste for symmetry. The jumble of* **naturalia** *and* **artificialia** *is accentuated by the accumulation of paintings within the painting, including works by Joos de Momper and Jan Brueghel, as well as Gerard David's* **Portrait of a Jeweller** *(below right).*

owners. Martin Lister's *Historiae Conchyliorum*, published in London between 1685 and 1692, has no fewer than a thousand plates of shells. A few years earlier the Jesuit, Father Filippo Buonanni, in response to another Jesuit, the legendary Father Athanasius Kircher, had published the first great book of shell engravings (*Ricreatione dell'Occhio e della Mente nell'Osservation' delle Chiocciole*, Rome, 1681), whose pages show objects made up of a patchwork of shells.

This was followed by a number of well-known publications in various countries of Europe, including *D'Amboinsche Rariteitkamer*, written in Dutch by the German Georg Rumph (published in 1705 three years after his death); *Index Testarum Conchyliorum* by the Italian Niccolò Gualtieri, published in Florence in 1742; *La Conchyliologie* by Antoine Dézallier d'Argenville (also 1742); while the Amsterdam apothecary Albert Seba devoted to the marvels of conchology no less than an entire large volume in the four-volume catalogue of his collections (the publication of which spread over more than thirty years). The magnificence of the plates, many of them forming grotesque faces, has rendered the work justly famous.

Each of these memorable books is groping towards a classification. Some attempt is made to reduce the diversity of forms, to break away from the tyranny of appearance; but for the most part the proposed classifications depend ultimately on the shape of the shells and the analogies that this suggests. (Antoine Schnapper explains: 'Since Aristotle, we have set out within a summary framework – Univalves, Turbinates, Bivalves – only a few poorly defined types: cowrie, whelk, murex, pen shell, conch, razor clam, turban shell, etc.') Dézallier d'Argenville begins by sketching out four typical forms, but ends up lost in a thicket of analogies. Even more than other objects in the natural sciences, the shell illustrates the fascinating dialectic between critical description and the deceptive pitfall, with the former leading inevitably to the latter.

Even after Linnaeus finally introduced his system of classification in 1758 (a date generally regarded as the moment of disenchantment, when a halt was put to magical or extravagant interpretations), the power of suggestion continued to infiltrate and the many names acquired by analogy to be preserved.

Most great curio cabinets had their conchological section, some better supplied than others. Erasmus, Rumph and the Tradescants had collections now long since dispersed; Mazarin's was valued at four thousand French livres; Gaston d'Orléans kept his shells in 'eighteen of the twenty-two drawers of a cedar and ebony cabinet, and in four boxes, not counting some large shells kept separately'. He had in all just over a thousand shells, excluding the small 'valueless' ones. Dumolinet devoted one of the six plates in the second part of *Le Cabinet de la Bibliothèque de Sainte-Geneviève* (Paris, 1692) to 'the most remarkable shells', now held by the Museum d'Histoire Naturelle in Paris; while the collection of Queen Louisa Ulrica of Sweden is still extant in the University of Uppsala.

The cabinets were supplied by dealers or agents about whom little information survives. Henry Coomans cites a shop in Paris known as 'Noah's Arke' as a supplier of *naturalia* in 1644, and mentions, after a gap of nearly a century, the 'Lovers of Neptune's Cabinet', a group of collectors meeting once a month at Dordrecht in Holland to discuss their hobby and possible swaps. Georg Rumph, whose work has been mentioned above, profited from his contacts on Amboina in the East Indies to trade with other collectors throughout Europe. Given the title of 'Plinius Indicus' ('the Indian Pliny'), he sold a major shell collection to Cosimo III de' Medici in 1682, and thus contributed indirectly to the Florentine devotion to the *studiolo* and the curio.

CHAPTER THREE THE MANNERIST SHELL

Ever since the time of Francis I de' Medici, nearly a century before Rumph, the shell had been an emblem of Florentine Mannerist culture. It was to be found in the 'rustic' scenery of the Pratolino gardens, in the décor of the Studiolo of the Palazzo Vecchio (Alessandro Allori's *Pearl Fishers*), in the alcove of the Boboli grotto, whose rock-crystal wall fountain, now encrusted with lime, originally reflected the lustre of shells. The shell could not fail to appeal to the Mannerist visionary. Barbara Jones notes: 'Nothing about a shell is quite as it appears to be at first glance'; it offers iridescence, reflection, chiaroscuro, convolution, mutability, impermanence. One level suggests enamel and feeds the Mannerist liking for hard, shiny, polished surfaces; another suggests water and is a true expression of the sea (just as Dumolinet, describing the nautilus, writes in the second part of his *Cabinet*: 'One is indebted to this fish, if it is true that it taught man the art of sailing; it is truly said that it takes pleasure in promenading the sea in its shell, as if in a natural gondola, and that is why it is given the name of nautilus.')

In the set of canvases covering the walls of the Studiolo of the Palazzo Vecchio, the *Pearl Fishers* forms part of a symbolic representation of the elements. The whole ensemble provides a small theatre of the world that could be grasped in reality or in imagination. In this alchemist's theatre, water, the element that represents changeability, has an essential place (with pearl and mother-of-pearl as the wonderfully contradictory tangible components of a silent dialectic). Similarly, Arcimboldo composed four heads for Rudolph II, intended to illustrate this dream of confounding reality by personifying water with a combination of pearls, fish and shells. Favourite token of princely melancholy, the shell retains something of its mythical provenance; the imprint of a corpse, it is the mute witness of a legendary origin, to which it refers in two different ways: through space, since it comes from far-away lands, presumed sites of primordial creation; and through time, as a remnant and relic of Noah's ark.

Such marvels of nature obviously require an appropriate framework. The rarity and symbolic power of *naturalia* in general, and shells in particular, appealed to the Mannerist obsession with framing and relief, to the taste for setting and architectural detail. In much the same category come the countless pictures showing the cabinets of enthusiasts. Antwerp, for example, established a whole sub-genre of painters who specialized in portraying these heaps of wealth, with or without their owners (Frans Francken the Younger, Adriaen van Stalbemt, Hieronymus Francken the Younger, Hendrik Staben and others). On oriental carpets or backgrounds of velvet were piled corals, ivories, reptile skulls, marble busts, globes, armillary spheres, nautiluses, spider crabs – sumptuous displays of possessions, illuminating 'the unexpected variety of earthly things', as a contemporary commentator wrote. But in the end, the obverse was always revealed: the vanity of laying up treasure on earth, a *memento mori*.

Seemingly intent on making a deliberately flamboyant statement, these two paintings bring together and develop some of the key elements of Mannerist attitudes: exoticism, the allegory of plenty, an erotic mythology and the taste for pearly, polished, iridescent flesh.

Above: *Alessandro Allori (1535–1607),* **Pearl Fishers,** *1570–72, Studiolo of the Palazzo Vecchio, Florence.*

Opposite: *Jacopo Zucchi (1541–c. 1589),* **The Treasures of the Sea,** *Galeria Borghese, Rome.*

Filippo Buonanni, Ricreatione dell'Occhio e della Mente nell'Osservation' delle Chiocciole, *Rome, 1681: frontispiece to Part IV. Clearly recalling Arcimboldo's composite faces of the previous century, this Baroque engraving is an early forerunner of the shell figures of the late-eighteenth and nineteenth centuries.*

PARTE · QVARTA

Si esprimono i Gusci de'Testacei, nella Parte seconda descritti.

Ricreatione
dell' Occhio e della Mente
nell' Osseruation' delle Chiocciole

29

The shell, a rock-like remnant or relic that expresses, in the truest sense, a living body, naturally conjures up analogy with the skull.

Thus it finds its place alongside symbols of human vanity, between the glass and the book and among other emblems of the fragility of earthly life.

Sebastian Stoskopf (1597–1657), **Still Life with Statuette and Shells,** *The Louvre, Paris.*

*Harmen van Steenwyck
(1612–c. 1656),* Vanitas,
National Gallery, London.

Albert Seba offered his Locupletissimi rerum naturalium thesauri... to the public in 1734. The subscription price for the four planned volumes, containing 449 engravings, was 160 guilders (the price after publication being 225 guilders). A de luxe edition with coloured plates cost 280 guilders, a record for the time. Seba himself never saw the complete edition, the last two volumes of which appeared after his death. Although the work covers the whole of the natural world, Seba shows a weakness for the richness and colourfulness of shells: 'What a charming spectacle this mixture of colours offers here, with its diversity of design and shape!' he writes in his preface. The plates remain among the most remarkable in the whole history of the illustrated book.

RITRATTO DEL MVSEO DI FERRANTE IMPERATO

In the plates that illustrate the classic books on the history of curiosities, such as (above) Ferrante Imperato's **Historia Naturale** *(1672)* or *(opposite)* Georg Rumph's **Thesaurus** *(1711), it is the* arrangement of the collection, the play of incongruity, that strikes the onlooker all the more forcibly with the passing of time, giving these improbable places an utterly surreal aspect.

THESAURUS
COCHLEARUM
CONCHARUM
CONCHYLIORUM
ET
MINERALIUM

LUGDUNI BATAVORUM, Excudit PETRUS VANDER AA, MDCCXI.

In the early eighteenth century, Levin Vincent stands at the end of one cultural period and the beginning of another. While the plate (left) from his Elenchus Tabularum... (1719) represents the ideal image of a cabinet of natural science, his engravings illustrating the contents of a collection show how aesthetic concerns and the taste for symmetry and harmony plainly outweigh the scientific interest: here shells and coral, far from being displayed as matchless rarities, are essentially motifs in a decorative scheme. The coral cabinet (above right) is from Wondertoneel der Natur (1706), the lobsters and other shellfish (below right) from Elenchus Tabularum....

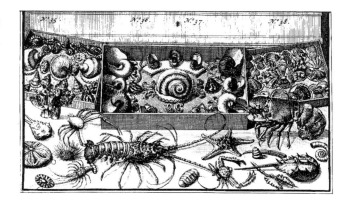

CHAPTER FOUR THE ROCAILLE FLOURISH

It has often been remarked that the fetishism of arrangement, the taste for an aesthetic layout of the collections in the curio cabinets (as can clearly be seen in the plates of Levin Vincent, for example), shifted these displays away from the realm of scientific knowledge and more towards the history of ornament, thereby accentuating the essential frivolousness of the objects exhibited.

With the development of maritime expeditions and colonial exploitation during the seventeenth century, imports of shells became so massive that the object lost its rarity value to become no more than an amusing oddity. From the end of the seventeenth century, curio cabinets could be found in grottoes. In the eighteenth century, it was not only grottoes, as urban expressions of rustic style, but also interiors and household items – such as a Dutch clock three metres high – that were smothered in shells. The eighteenth century turned to the shell both as a decorative material, covering walls and surfaces with a rough, irregular finish, and as an inspirational motif, effectively giving its name to a style: the Rocaille, precursor of the Rococo. As the exotic and magical qualities receded, the aesthetic and tactile values grew.

The style is typified by the shell. Rocaille (literally 'rockwork') is defined in the 1771 edition of the *Trévoux Dictionary* as: 'Assemblage of several shells with unmatched and rough-polished stones, placed around rocks and in imitation of them. It is a composition of rustic architecture, imitating natural rocks, and is made from pitted stones, shells and petrifactions of various colours, as can be seen in grottoes that contain fountains and their pools.'

The shell by its very shape, roughness and unevenness of surface was the perfect instrument of the Rocaille's aesthetic of instability. In a 1736 composition on the theme, Boucher piled up cone shells and whelks in an assemblage that exaggerated the effect of the material, the whorls and improbable excrescences, and skewed the design at an angle that gave it the look of a palm tree inherited from Bernini. Similarly, the *Mercure de France* of March 1734 contains an article praising an issue of engravings by Juste-Aurèle Meissonnier which, according to Fiske Kimball, was among the very first to welcome the appearance of the Rocaille:

'A suite of Engravings has appeared, in the manner of Stefano della Bella, that should arouse the curiosity of the Public and Collectors of the finest taste. They are Fountains, Cascades, Ruins, Rockworks and Shells, fragments of Architecture that make for bizarre, singular and picturesque effect, by their exciting and extraordinary shapes, where one part often has nothing to do with another, without the subject appearing less rich and attractive.'

The same period saw the French trader Edme François Gersaint offer collectors a choice of shells ('everything fine and rare that I could find in the genre') that he had sought out in Holland. In his *Catalogue raisonné de coquilles et autres curiosités naturelles* (Paris, 1736), he wrote: 'Shells form a felicitous group, and the sight of them may inspire lofty ideas as to form in architects and sculptors, and even in painters.' The object, although still an exotic import, was distinguished not for its rarity, but rather for its plastic qualities (which are also highlighted in the *magnum opus* of Dézallier d'Argenville already referred to, *La Conchyliologie*, published six years after Gersaint's catalogue).

The shell miraculously combines all the aspects of the Rocaille aesthetic, and of the Rococo – 'a lyrical conception of humanity, a response to all that is transitory and fugacious, a calligraphy of farewell', as evoked by Cyril Connolly. First and foremost the asymmetry, or the serpentine motion that Hogarth found so pleasing: 'The eye is rejoiced to see the object turned, and shifted, so as to vary these uniform appearances.... Simplicity, without variety, is wholly insipid, and at best does only not displease; but when variety is joined to it, then it pleases, because it enhances the pleasure of variety, by giving the eye the power of enjoying it with ease' (*The Analysis of Beauty*, 1753). The Rocaille, following in the tradition of 'Gothic' irregularity, of Mannerism and Borromini, dismisses the balances and axes that are the architectural inspiration of ornament. What we see is 'an invasion of architecture by decoration until ... decoration creates its own architecture' (Connolly). The rock, the coral and the shell replace the acanthus and the olive.

The design and contours of the shell respond to the Rocaille liking for circular forms, for the asymmetrical cut, for outlines and sinuous borders, whose echo is to be found in the scrolls, shields and cartouches typical of the period. The shell's texture, ruggedness and plasticity go on to suggest petrifaction and sedimentation.

A rocky world is thus enjoined, all quirks and chances, bumps and hollows, a world of caverns and reliefs, for which the grotto is a favoured means of expression. The grotto stimulates an architecture of fantasy (to which we shall return). Joan Evans found one of the earliest examples in seventeenth-century Venice in the palace of Count Giacomo Cavazza (a saloon described by Molmenti as 'an open space converted into a grotto, with incrustations on its walls formed of pebbles and sea-shells').

The shell is intrinsically associated with the essential element of the Rocaille: water. Cascades, ripples, whirlpools, jets and trickles play and break upon the furrowed surfaces of shells, or else caress them and make them sparkle. Twin poles of a vision whose games seem inexhaustible and endlessly fascinating – as if the solid substance, the glitter, the transparency and hardness of a shell were only the effect of airborne vapours, froth, liquefied aromas, congealed fluidity: a transitory state between two moments of change in a material in constant motion. (After a gap of several centuries, a similar game in the relationship of water and the shell, with its own grammar, appears in the work of Filippo De Pisis, a well-known enthusiast for the Rococo.)

It has often been said that the Rocaille was 'the age of porcelain'. The shell with its inner and outer layers, translucent and pearly, with the delicacy of its tones and the fineness of its polish, once again espouses the taste of an era. What is sought here is a brilliance of sheen linked to an indefinable softness of colour, a contradictory marriage of crystal hardness and absolute fragility. There is a fascination in transparency, in the frailty of a material transfused with light that seems about to splinter into fragments. At the heart of the Rocaille lies a further fascination in transitory things and fleeting feelings. Hence the proliferation of snuff-boxes, vanity cases, trinket boxes and caskets – little witty objects formed as delicately as a shell held in the hand. This did not escape Charles de Brosses, the Encyclopédiste, who wrote: 'The Gothic taste [namely the Rocaille] is tiny, delicate, detailed, and suitable for small objects, but never for big ones.' The shell with its minuteness, delicacy and detailing is the ultimate expression of the Rocaille flourish.

LIVRE D'ORNEMENS
Inventés & Dessines
PAR J.O. MEISSONNIER
ARCHITECTE, DESSINATEUR
de la Chambre & Cabinet
DU ROI.

Laureolli Sculp.

Meissonnier Archit.t in.

avec privilege du Roi.

Laureolli Sculp.

Opposite: *Juste-Aurèle Meissonnier (c. 1695–1750)*, **Livre d'ornemens**, *1734.*

Together with Gilles-Marie Oppenord and François de Cuvilliés, Meissonnier was the most celebrated representative of the Rocaille. Originally from Turin, he was primarily a goldsmith, and his major works demand attention through the controlled madness of their ornamentation. These two vignettes show how the asymmetry, ruggedness, convexities and concavities of the shell 'contaminate' every form in the world of the Rocaille.

Jean-Baptiste Pigalle (1714–1785), **Holy-Water Stoups**, *1745, Saint-Sulpice, Paris.*

The holy-water stoups of Saint-Sulpice epitomize the history and fortune of the shell theme. Originally presented by the Venetian Republic to François I as objects of great rarity, the two giant clam shells were entrusted to the skilled hands of Pigalle in 1745 by Louis XV. The sculptor gave them asymmetrical supports, distantly recalling the rocks of Bernini's Four Rivers fountain in Rome and transforming them into emblems of a totally new aesthetic.

Probably made (according to Marianne Roland-Michel) for Gabriel Huquier, the engraver and printseller of most of Jacques de Lajoue's designs, this wonderful screen (c. 1740) is divided into three parts on each side of its six leaves, representing the elements of air, earth and water. Shells proliferate in the lowest register, along with rustic ornaments, mosses and corals.

Opposite: *Personifying the Rocaille aesthetic, Jacques de Lajoue (1686–1761) used countless scenes of parks and fountains as pretexts for arabesques and scrolls. In this painting, the cupids are taken directly from Boucher. The composition* *recurs frequently in Lajoue's work: a huge shell embedded in a wall and extended into falls and jets of water – the solid extending into the liquid.*

Above: *François Boucher,* **Rocaille** *and* **Leda,** *engraved by Claude Duflos the Younger, c. 1736.*

Boucher's bold visual manifesto of the Rocaille style (left) is distinguished by its zigzag composition, its asymmetry and the accumulation of all kinds of shells, corals *and seaweeds, even the basin of the fountain being in the form of a shell. The story of Leda and the Swan (right) takes up the same elements, using the mythological scene as a pretext for unrestrained invention.*

Premier

FRONTISPICE.

LA
CONCHYLIO
LOGIE.

R.etouché et conduit par Jac.
De Favanne.

INVENTÉ par FRANÇOIS
BOUCHER.

Gra. à l'Eau F. par Chedel et
Ter. au Bu. par J.Robert.

Left: *A few years after the publication of his graphic manifesto on the Rocaille, Boucher was persuaded to design the frontispiece of Dézallier d'Argenville's* **La Conchyliologie** *(1742). This celebration of the passion for shells enjoyed enormous success and was reprinted several times in the course of the eighteenth century.*

Opposite: *The 'dwarf Couvelier', as contemporary accounts referred to him (his first appointment was as Court Dwarf), was one of the most brilliant interpreters of Rocaille ornamentation. François de Cuvilliés (1695–1768), chief architect to the Bavarian court from 1725, radically transformed the face of Munich, notably in the gardens, parade rooms (Reiche Zimmer) and*

48

theatre of the Residenz, the Antiquarium and the façade of the Theatine Church. His finest achievement is probably the hunting-box of Amalienburg (1734–39) in the park at Nymphenburg. Beginning in 1738, he published almost five hundred plates of his engravings of 'inventions', caprices, cartouches, ceilings, furniture, etc. Le Livre Nouveau de Morceaux de fantaisie à divers usages, *published c. 1740, from which this plate is taken, consists, like all Cuvilliés's other 'books', of six loose sheets of plates, held together with a piece of string.*

F. de Cuvilliés. In. et. del. C. P. S. CM. C. A. de Lespilliez. sc.

CHAPTER FIVE FANTASTIC ARCHITECTURE

The dark alchemical currents of the Renaissance had already made the grotto, and its accretions, a subject of scholarly investigation. Porphyry's *De Antro Nympharum* of the third century AD, a key text of Neo-Platonism, was constantly reprinted after 1518, stimulating the philosophical and alchemical thinking of the Renaissance. For his part, Leon Battista Alberti, another pillar of thought of the age, underlines all the dramatic character, scenic quality and manysidedness of the grotto. He immediately conjures up the artificial grottoes of the ancients, bristling with '*minuti pezzi di pomice*' (tiny chips of pumice), fragments of volcanic ash and oyster shells, and daubed with green wax in imitation of the mossy slime always present in moist grottoes. The grotto with its evocation of shadowy and archaic powers is also an archaeological phenomenon: it directly recalls the nymphaea of Pompeii, mysterious Roman buildings in which tuff and lava are mingled with coral, shells, branches and every kind of debris in a powerful combination of reject and relic. Throughout the sixteenth century, Italy witnessed the 'rustic inventions' of Pirro Ligorio for the Villa d'Este at Tivoli, the grottoes for the Villa Medici at Castello (1567) and for the villa at Pratolino (1570), while at Schloss Ambras, near Innsbruck, the Hapsburgs furnished themselves with 'sea-dragon lairs', and in France Bernard Palissy was constructing his extraordinary aquatic transformation scenes.

Eugenio Battisti wrote: 'The grotto has in it something static and timeless.' It is the direct antithesis of the dome; for while the latter fixes the gaze and draws it along the lines of light in an enclosed and abstract space, the grotto offers the spectator a glimpse of the depths, a shadowy setting, a deepening darkness in a confusion of crannies, clefts and protrusions, revealing broken relief where the shell catches a last glimmer of light, scatters a few glints, and provides a rough but at the same time well-ordered image of the material.

Claude d'Urfé, French ambassador to the Holy See, then governor of the royal children, imported this aspect of the Italian style into France, adding (in 1551) to his château in the Loire an impressive grotto, punctuated by arcades and columns and entirely encrusted with small stones and shells. As in the Boboli grotto, monument to the taste for the unfinished, where the incomplete *Slaves* of Michelangelo seem to be struggling to free themselves from the rocky mass that holds them, the grotto of the Bastie d'Urfé contains low reliefs and statues embedded in an inlay of stones and shells. A century ahead it foreshadows, in a seemingly irresistible move towards orderliness and 'high' taste, the Grotto of Thetis conceived for Versailles by Charles Perrault and built around 1665 by his brother Claude in collaboration with Le Brun. It was destroyed in 1684 when Mansart was constructing the north wing of the château, but two records of it survive: the superb engravings of 1676 by Jean Le Pautre for *Le Cabinet du Roi*, and the verse description by La Fontaine in *Les Amours de Psiché et de Cupidon* (1669):

> *Of choice Materials are the Roof and Floor:*
> *Shells, by the Waves disgorg'd along the Shore;*
> *Or Pebbles, which in Earth's deep Womb are found,*
> *Dispos'd in gay Compartments, glitter round.*
> *High o'er six columns, similar in Size,*
> *Six rustic Masks (their Aspect furious rise):*
> *Phantasms of Art, with Eyes cast wildly down,*
> *They, from a Niche, on all who enter, frown.*
> *Beauties unnumber'd in the Niche appear...*

(as first translated into English by John Lockman, *The Loves of Cupid and Psyche*, London, 1744).

Mansart had the idea of another 'rustic' grouping of which some traces remain: it was the nymphaeum of Maisons-Laffitte, populated with dolphins, Tritons, grotesque masks and sea-horses, originally located at the entrance to the château's stables. It is just one example of the many shell edifices that followed in the seventeenth century: the earliest is thought to be that at Issy-les-Moulineaux built for Queen Margot (Margaret of Valois) at the very beginning of the century. In 1635 the hydraulic engineer Thomas Francini designed the Wideville grotto, whose façade closely resembles that of the Medici fountain in the Jardins du Luxembourg, and whose interior is entirely covered in shells arranged in geometric or anthropomorphic patterns.

It has been noted that the same model occurs in the architecture of the Ombreval nymphaeum, near Lyons; although that of Jouy-en-Josas, built in 1680 in the form of a cave punctuated by arches, is closer to the Bastie d'Urfé.

The fashion was by no means confined to France. The Prince Bishop of Salzburg, for example, in 1615 conceived a Neptune's grotto studded with shells and furnished with two water organs. But it was above all in England that the passion for shells took hold. That excellent chronicler of the unusual John Aubrey cites the eccentric figure of Thomas Bushell, seal bearer to Francis Bacon and 'greatest Master of the Art of running in Debt (perhaps) in the world'. Never short of wonderful ideas, he hit one day on the notion of digging a grotto at Enstone in Oxfordshire 'to sitt and read, or contemplate' under a décor of stalactites and shells, opposite 'a Neptune, neatly cutt in wood, holding his Trident in his hand, and ayming with it at a Duck which perpetually turned round with him, and a Spanniel swimming after her…'.

Thomas Bushell's grotto, long vanished from sight, was soon followed by the oldest-surviving and best-known example of this kind of edifice in England: that built by the fourth Duke of Bedford at Woburn Abbey in about 1630. With one side opening on to the garden through three arches, it is usually attributed to Isaac de Caus, although Horace Walpole spoke of a grotto by Inigo Jones. The vault is covered with repetitive geometric patterns, while in each lunette a mask of Neptune is surrounded by mermaids and boys on dolphins. The only other English work of comparable age to the Woburn Abbey decoration can still be seen at Skipton Castle in North Yorkshire, although it has been substantially altered over the years.

The following century unquestionably marks the apogee of the passion for shells; and England was the favoured stage for the craze. Continental Europe was not entirely left out, however: among other well-known examples may be mentioned the grotto and its furnishings at Sanssouci (1763), near Potsdam; the Echarcon nymphaeum in the Ile de France, where rocks and foliage conduct a dialogue; the parks of La Mogère (*c.* 1770) or of La Mosson, near Montpellier; and finally the shell cottage of the royal park at Rambouillet (1779), not far from Marie-Antoinette's famous dairy, to which Hubert Robert lent a hand. But these royal or noble instances can not be compared with the effects of the sudden frenzy that struck England around 1730. Barbara Jones writes: 'For about twenty years (and sporadically after that) duchesses, bankers, poets, Mrs Delany, and Mr Pope gathered shells on the shore, begged them from travellers, scrambled for them at sales and bought whole shipments when they had to…. Rooms, caves and whole suites of underground apartments, furnished with baths and marble seats, carpeted with moss for special occasions and tinkling perpetually with cascades, were entirely encrusted with shells and spar in half the great houses in England.'

England had already had its literary gardening enthusiasts in the seventeenth century. After Francis Bacon and his essay *Of Gardens*, John Evelyn, diarist and polymath, became interested in the gardens of Europe, made one for himself, and subsequently wrote a treatise on forest-trees, *Sylva*, and expounded on the theme of salads in his *Acetaria*. In the eighteenth century, Alexander Pope took up the notion of the picturesque and his shell temple at Twickenham was doubtless part of the fashion that seized the country. It was a strange octagonal dome resting on eight rusticated columns curving in towards the base, as if bending under the weight of the load they had to bear.

A steady series of grottoes and retreats marks the rest of the century. The next was built by a certain Thomas Goldney of Bristol, begun in 1737, and its dramatic, not to say terrifying, aspects are highlighted by Barbara Jones – shifting light and water, sound and shadow, tortuous rocks and petrified life.

In contrast, the grotto at Goodwood Park in West Sussex (1739) is scintillating and distinguished for the elegant way it is picked out and the 'mathematical precision' of its shellwork decorations. Sarah, second Duchess of Richmond, and her daughters used thousands upon thousands of shells for the purpose. The walls are cut out in niches and alcoves, or divided into panels, with places for urns, and decorated with an infinite variety of rigorously precise stars, acanthus leaves and circles.

Only a few of the subsequent eccentric architectural efforts will be mentioned. In the *cottage orné* at Carton in County Kildare, Ireland, a skylighted shell room, owed to Emilia Mary, daughter of the Duchess of Richmond, in the middle of the century, is an excellent example of the lengths to which this aesthetic could go. It was like a game of patience, primarily an antidote to boredom, an activity that was at the same time unnecessary and demanding: the very precision is a sign of futility. This kind of work was mostly carried on by ladies who showed off their shell marquetry just as they might show off their knitting or a dress. We can still be touched by the tenacity of these busy little hands, the patience of these members of the idle leisured class, devoid of the least talent, but resolute, stubborn, tenacious in their determination not to be bored and in their blind desire to be creative, as expressed by the extreme regularity of the patterns, the ingenuity of the designs and the redeeming abstraction of someone who has not really found the right register for expression.

In the shell cottage at Carton, twigs and shellwork are combined in geometrical arrangements. Barbara Jones also notes wool, coral, mirrors, tufa and tiles as materials, along with birds' eggs, minerals, pine cones and cedar cones. Shellwork was not therefore merely an occupation for women with little to do: it became one of the strongest expressions of the British genius for recycling, for the art of refuse disposal, for making everything into a trifling relic, and for finding a use for waste.

Perhaps the finest evocation of a way of life centred on the collection and display of shells comes in the recently published correspondence of Mrs Delany, an expert in shellwork and friend of Handel, Walpole and Fanny Burney, whose life embraces most of the eighteenth century (1700–1788). In September 1732 she ornamented a grotto for the Bishop of Killala in Ireland: 'Do you not wish yourself extended on the beach *gathering shells*, listening to Phill while she sings at her work, or joining in the conversation, always attended with cheerfulness? Perhaps you had rather rise by seven and walk to the grotto with your bag of shells, and a humble servant by your side, helping you up the hill and saying pretty things to you as you walk? Though maybe you choose to be at work in the grotto shewing the elegancy of your fancy, praising your companion's works, and desiring an approbation for what you have finished? If this is too fatiguing, it is likely you would prefer working or reading till dinner, after that eating nuts and walking to gather mushrooms.'

Towards the middle of the century, Mrs Delany decorated another grotto at Delville, near Dublin, while also covering in shells garden pots, book-ends and even a chandelier, which was soon destroyed by damp. Her shellwork came between making superb paper mosaics of flowers (now in the British Museum), harp recitals, painting watercolours, drawing and gathering a meticulous collection of marine rarities which were endlessly polished, scraped and burnished before finding their place in the drawers of a purpose-built cabinet. Towards 1860 the hobby lost its appeal and she turned to needlework and botany.

Another excellent player in the history of this hidden-away art in the eighteenth century is identified by Barbara Jones: 'Josiah Lane, with a varying number of sons or brothers, came from Fonthill or Tisbury or Westbury in Wiltshire, did the grotto at Fonthill, and was also stated in later county guides to have done the grottoes at Pain's Hill, Oatlands, Norbiton House at Kingston, and Wardour.'

Oatlands, in Surrey, destroyed in January 1948, must have been one of the most impressive grottoes of the period. It cost about £40,000 and took five, or possibly twelve, years to finish. The Duchess of York took meals there and played with her dogs and monkeys. In 1815, the victory at Waterloo was celebrated there in a setting glowing with a thousand flames, the crystal chandeliers lighting up the stalactites of white spar and the encrustations of white and pink shells.

Ascot House (Berkshire), Bowood (Wiltshire), Wimborne St Giles (Dorset), Curraghmore (Waterford) and Acton Burnell (Shropshire) are among the many other places examined by Barbara Jones in her *magnum opus* on eccentric buildings which included, or still preserve, shell decorations going back to the eighteenth century.

As the industrial revolution approached, the very appearance of the grottoes changed. They lost their shimmer, their reflections, the glint of mirror-glass, the lustre of white or pink shells, the sparkle of feldspar and quartz. Emphasis was given to shadowy corners, to the dramatic, to a theatricality of mystery, of secret rooms and concealed passageways more suited to the Gothick taste.

At the same time, the shell grotto became a middle-class attraction, an adjunct to the garden, a minor domestic exoticism that could be acquired without too much effort for a country house or a small public park, or could be fitted out as a tea-room or a watering place. Perhaps the last gasp of the passion for shells of the eighteenth century may be seen in the shell decoration done by the Misses Parminter for the octagon at their poetic house A la Ronde, near Exmouth, Devon. As Olive Cook and Edwin Smith explained in the 1952 *Saturday Book*: 'But the most ambitious use of shells and seaweeds is surely the decoration of the octagon at A la Ronde. The Misses Jane and Mary Parminter had travelled in Italy and aspired to re-create in their Regency House some of the features of San Vitale, Ravenna. The walls of the central hall are encrusted … with mosaics, executed not in glass and stone, but in shells, seaweeds and feathers, all gathered with remarkable industry from the Devonshire coast.' The shell mosaics in short offered nothing more than an insular version of a Byzantine church.

The Bastie d'Urfé was built in 1535 by Claude d'Urfé in the heart of the Forez region of central France that was later made famous by his grandson Honoré as the setting of his pastoral romance L'Astrée, a key work in seventeenth-century French literature. Giants and Tritons add emphasis to the walls and pilasters of a great grotto room, every part of which is completely covered with shells and pebbles. In the niches that line the walls, the shell motif is taken up again, following a classical model.

Left: *Together with those of Issy-les-Moulineaux and Maisons-Laffitte, the nymphaeum of Jouy-en-Josas is one of the oldest-surviving examples of the 'reinvention' of these magical places. It comprises a multiple-vaulted cave covered with shells arranged in geometrical patterns or forming mythological figures.*

Vue du fonds de la Grotte de Versailles, ornée de trois Groupes de marbre blanc, qui representent le Soleil au milieu des Nymphes de Thetis, et ses chevaux pensez par des Tritons.

Prospectus Cryptæ Interioris Versaliarum, ubi sol inter Nymphas Thetidis, et ejus equi cum Tritonibus, statuæ marmoreæ exhibentur.

Right: *The Wideville grotto was constructed by Thomas Francini in 1635, a few years after he had designed the Medici fountain in the Jardins du Luxembourg in Paris. Their façades are very similar, both having four rusticated attached columns supporting a segmental pediment.*

Opposite: *All that remains of the Grotto of Thetis at Versailles, conceived by Charles Perrault and built by his brother Claude c. 1665, are a celebration in verse by La Fontaine and some engravings by Jean Le Pautre in* Le Cabinet du Roi, *published in 1676. This view shows the depths of the grotto with its three groups of white marble representing the sun, Thetis and her nymphs, and her horses being held by Tritons.*

Built by François Mansart (1598–1666), the nymphaeum of Maisons-Laffitte originally stood at the entrance to the château's stables, which explains the motif of stucco Tritons and sea-horses that stand out against the background of shell-mosaic.

Shell pavilion in the park of the château of Rambouillet, second half of the eighteenth century.

Along with the famous dairy which Louis XVI had built for Marie-Antoinette, this pavilion is one of the most celebrated follies of the eighteenth century. Reflecting the modish contemporary taste for a return to nature, it was built by the Duc de Penthièvre for his widowed daughter-in-law, the Princesse de Lamballe. The thatched roof and rustic exterior give no hint of the sumptuous inlay of shells covering the interior walls.

Right: *Schloss Pommersfelden was built between 1711 and 1718 by the architect Johann Dientzenhofer for Lothar Franz von Schönborn, Archbishop Elector of Mainz. Centred around an impressive staircase and containing a marble saloon, superb stuccoed ceilings and a cabinet of mirrors, it is one of the very finest examples of German Baroque architecture. The Gartensaal, giving on to the park, contains numerous statues, including the personification of water, set against walls smothered in plasterwork, splinters of glass and shells.*

Opposite: *The park of Nymphenburg, outside Munich, contains pavilions built for the Wittelsbachs in the eighteenth century. One of them, dedicated to death, is crazed with false cracks and crevices and encrusted with shells, rocks and pebbles.*

Teatro Massimo dell' Isola Bella ————   Grand Théatre de L'Isle Belle ——

Count Carlo Borromeo began his transformation of the arid rock of Isola Bella – originally named 'Isola Isabella' in honour of his wife – in about 1630. He never saw the finished gardens, which took some forty years to complete. The whole island, according to one admiring traveller, was 'like the ancient Gardens of the Hesperides', carpeted with ornamental flower-beds and cut into ten terraces rising to more than a hundred feet above the lake. The shell appears as a leitmotiv throughout the island, as ornament, inlay work and sculpture.

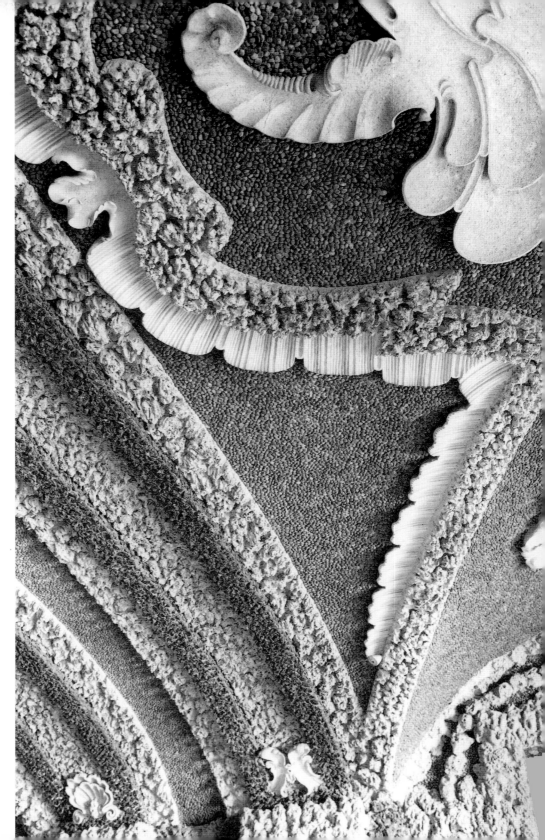

Probably designed by Isaac de Caus, the shell room at Woburn Abbey dates from about 1630. Consisting of a large vaulted hall, its walls covered with bands of rustication, it is inhabited by mermaids, dolphins, sea gods and Neptune masks. The play of light on the shells covering the imitation waves gives the illusion of movement.

*The octagon at A la Ronde
in Devon was the work
of the Misses Jane and
Mary Parminter at the end
of the eighteenth century.
The mosaics of shells on
the walls alternate with
motifs of birds done in
feathers. The whole
presents a splendid
monument to the glory
of the work of such ladies,
evidence (as Barbara
Jones has written) of a
'vanished zenith of
feminine elegance'.*

CHAPTER SIX KITSCH AND GROTTO FURNITURE

As ornament, the shell quietly experienced its moments of glory and eclipse. Joan Evans – setting aside the phenomenon of Compostela – noted that the shell had been curiously little used in medieval decoration, except for a page of an illuminated manuscript by Cybo of Hyères dating from 1390. It is no surprise that the nineteenth century, always eager to find medieval or Gothic echoes, was not a high point for the motif. Whether firstly with Viollet le Duc, the French Troubadour style or William Morris, or later with Art Nouveau, nineteenth-century ornament is based mainly on the swaying, curving lines of plant forms, embodying networks of tendrils and interlacing foliage.

James Laver wrote in 1957: 'So far as the use of the shell-motif in decorative art is concerned, this might be thought to be the end of the story.' Clouded by the medieval revivalism of the nineteenth century, he was blind to the resurgence of the motif during the twentieth, paying heed only to 'the austerities of modern decoration', to the detriment of the Neo-Rococo and Neo-Romanticism whose significance has been much more widely recognized in recent years.

There was, however, one exception, when the shell staged what Laver calls 'a curious revenge' as part of Regency taste. Having been crowded out by the sphinxes, classical trophies and all the other devices of the Empire style, it reappeared in a fantastic form

in what Laver terms 'Pavilion furniture', that is the picturesque and
sometimes bizarre objects conceived for the Royal Pavilion in Brighton at
the start of the nineteenth century. The Prince Regent, the future George
IV, 'had a whole set of chairs and tables made entirely in the shell form,
the seats of the chairs being one huge flat shell carved in wood and
painted to represent the natural appearance of the scallop.' In this royal
whim lie, according to the historian, a foretaste – or a powerful catalyst
at least – for the 'seaside' aspect, for the kitsch knick-knacks that the
Victorians would develop, and which would soon be stocked by any self-
respecting seaside kiosk. The sale catalogue of a firm of the period lists
'at most reasonable prices', shell paperweights, shell purses, shell
brooches, shell hair-grips, shell pincushions, shell mirrors, shell trinket
boxes, shell picture-frames, and even shell crucifixes and shell shrines –
all burnished to look like ivory. Not to mention the little figures under
glass domes, the miniature churches and the landscapes made of shells
and other strange creatures in which souvenir sellers abound. The shell
at the end of its history became the exact opposite of what it initially
represented: a cheap medium of popular art, the commonest exoticism
of all, a three-dimensional substitute for the postcard.

Curiously, the Prince Regent's shell furniture receives no mention
by the chroniclers of whimsicality when they deal with the one subject
of importance for the shell motif in the nineteenth century, namely grotto
furniture. This unusual type of furniture, in carved and painted wood and
drawing on the whole repertoire of Tritons, scallop shells and sea-horses,

was presumed for many years to be of eighteenth-century origin because of the gracefulness of its form. With rare exceptions (including a design by Chippendale in 1762 in the third edition of *The Gentleman and Cabinet-Maker's Director*), this is not the case. The typical manufacture, as Bruce Newman and Alastair Duncan have shown, indicates a later origin. ('Its construction is conceived and executed in a rudimentary and often unsteady manner that is contrary to the rich traditions of eighteenth-century cabinetry. Its components are not joined in the conventional manner to which even the most adventurous furniture of the period conformed. Wooden pegs are absent; in their place are commercial screws that secure the backrest to the seat…. To compensate for the absence of doweling, reinforcing struts have often been applied to the undersides of seats and tabletops. Further examination reveals that the structural components were finished by machine, rather than manually.')

These creations of a latter-day, though constrained, Brustolon could have come only from Venice. Their creation in the 1880s is attributed to the firm of Pauly, a renowned supplier of quality Venetian glass and crafts, and long established under the arcades of the Procuratie Nuove (it now produces only glass and mirror-ware). A second firm, Remi, seems to have been active in the same field. Newman and Duncan write: 'Grotto furniture is comprised of four basic components: scalloped shells, sea horses, dolphins and triton horns. Combinations vary.' The furniture was carved, fluted and distorted. Most was finished in a lacquered silver leaf heightened with an overlay of metallic brownish gilt glaze, with the whole simulating the nacreous secretions inside real shells. Without quite attaining the astonishing Baroque of Andrea Brustolon's furniture that adorns this or that Venetian palace, this grotto furniture undoubtedly represents the most extreme, if not sole, variant in the nineteenth century of the shell as a decorative motif – fantasy furniture that is rescued from being mere kitsch by the faded fire of the gilding and the silver leaf. It made a comeback in one of the most publicized decorative schemes of the twentieth century, at a key moment for the motif's revival.

The Vow of Louis XIII, decorative panel, mid-eighteenth century. The ornamental excess in this panel immediately brings to mind the style and workmanship of the Nevers glasshouse, where little figures and decorative scenes were fashioned from glass rods in the seventeenth and eighteenth centuries. There is the same expression of naive piety, the same desire to saturate the space, the same triumph of the minuscule.

Some examples of figures and objects in shellwork, dating from the eighteenth century, before the massive proliferation of such items in the centuries that followed: a couple in the local costume of the Guérande region (Loire-Atlantique); a miniature dressing-table with drawers for pins (30 cm high, 23 cm wide); a little gardener in front of two pots of flowers; a pair of birds in shades of pink; and (opposite) a rare example of a 'three-dimensionalized' architectural fantasy in the style of Lajoue with minutely detailed inlay.

Three stages in the development of grotto furniture. A fanciful English model (right) proposed by Thomas Chippendale in the eighteenth century (from his chapter on 'Designs for Garden Seats' in The Gentleman and Cabinet-Maker's Director*), and* (opposite) *its French* incarnation towards the end of the same century: *grotto armchair, 88 cm high.* Below: *An example by Pauly of Venice, which made countless variations of the model and distributed its gilded or silvered furniture throughout the length and breadth of nineteenth-century Europe.*

Opposite: *Bowl and dish, Chantilly ware, mid-eighteenth century (Sèvres, Musée National de la Céramique).*

Above: *Four nineteenth-century Paris porcelain cups, clam-shaped with handles imitating coral.*

Above right: *Nineteenth-century Paris teapot and cream jug (13 x 13 cm and 10 x 10 cm).*

Right: *French, nineteenth-century barbotine bonbonnière (28 cm high, 24 cm wide).*

Barbotine, a paste of kaolin clay employed as a slip, was widely used in the nineteenth century, allowing the production of the richly coloured decoration that reflected the taste of the age. Although most vases and pots of the period carried floral motifs, the theme of the shell was also very popular.

Opposite: *Small porcelain vase in the form of a shell (13 cm high), Minton, barbotine, 1865.*

Left: *Porcelain jug in the form of a Triton holding a shell (35 cm high), Minton, barbotine, 1870.*

CHAPTER SEVEN THE BAROQUE DREAM

Helena Rubinstein, the cosmetics queen, had a mansion at 24 Quai de Béthune on the Ile Saint-Louis in Paris rebuilt by the architect and designer Louis Süe. Work began in 1934 and when it was finished in 1937 it received an award as the building of the year. The mansion provided a setting for the innumerable items that the owner had collected – from Byzantium to the flea market, as one harsh commentator put it. In a salon that became symbolic were displayed, under Pavel Tchelitchew's sequinned portrait of the mistress of the house, a superb shell-settee, a Venetian blackamoor, pieces of Indian furniture and various examples of African and Oceanic art. This 'offensive of Baroque taste', as a critic of the time called it, combined all the features of a changing taste in a certain society, whose influence has long been underestimated.

It may be linked with another memorable setting: the one imposed by Carlos de Beistegui, starting on his career as a patron of the grand taste, on the apartment he commissioned from Le Corbusier on the Champs-Elysées in the 1930s. Stark spaces, huge plate-glass windows, terraces and split levels structured by the architect were counterbalanced by vast mirrors and

Napoleon III ottomans, ormolu wall-brackets and sliding chandeliers (they slid along hidden rails), a Rococo commode and a Dresden blackamoor, curtains of pale-blue velvet and porcelain figurines. A spiral staircase led to the roof-garden with a finely kept lawn, a stone fireplace and *trompe-l'oeil* furniture. A geometry of illusion gave the lie to the austere and restrained vocabulary of the master of modern architecture and produced one of the most exuberant settings imaginable. The explanation given later by Jean-Michel Frank was that, in a brief spell of a year or two that we have now forgotten – between the time that work on the structure of the apartment had finished and the moment when it was necessary to decide on the furnishings – Modernism had for some become 'as *démodé* as Art Nouveau'. The ethos of Austerity, Cubism, Functionalism – precursors of the concept of 'less is more' – the brutalism of materials, the self-denying vocabulary and its rapid debasement had in the end transformed the expression of the modern into a new conformism. In institutional terms, the division in France came between the Union des Artistes Modernes, bringing together the major figures of the minimalist aesthetic, and the Société des Artistes Décorateurs, some of whose members (André Arbus, Jacques Adnet, Jean-Charles Moreux) were increasingly open to the assertion of new values: the use of precious materials, the extolling of technical mastery and virtuoso craftsmanship, the return to the treasury of classical forms, to memory, to metaphor, to flights of fantasy, to dreaming. This might be regarded as a distant reflection of the values of Surrealism, but that would be a misreading of the breadth of the new aesthetic trend of which examples can be found throughout Europe among writers, art dealers, painters, interior designers, photographers and their followers. What is being expressed here is a simple preference for ornamentation, accompanied by the revival of a decorative register that would remain fashionable, except during the war years, until the beginning of the 1960s. One of its key motifs, along with palms, candlesticks and blackamoors, was the shell.

As avowed ironists and determined nostalgics, always in search of the bizarre and the sensational, many writers and artists rejected the taboo cast upon ornamentation by modern art and mischievously turned back to forms of expression condemned by Modernism. They allowed themselves to dream of Victoriana, of Baroque and Rococo. They revived an age-old tradition of eccentricity, and often did so in the most outrageous manner. In England the Sitwells – Edith, Osbert and Sacheverell – fought fiercely for this new non-purism. Osbert Sitwell's decorative scheme in 1931 for his house in London's Carlyle Square piled up Victorian kitsch on Neapolitan Baroque. Sacheverell wrote many books on German and Neapolitan Rococo, on South American Baroque, on all the minor and forgotten arts. Edith, posing as a Gothic gargoyle, declaimed her tortured poetry and sent her friends photographs of her hand holding a shell.

Of the 1930s Martin Battersby dispassionately states: 'They were as unashamed in their preference for ornament as in their fondness for gin.' It is easy to identify some of the factors at work behind the Neo-Rococo: a natural liking for complexity, the influence of Italy as the eternal contrast to England, a confessed nostalgia for the 'bad taste' of earlier generations. There was also, as Battersby noted, the economic factor, in that Victorian or Regency objects, despised and rejected as they were, were easily obtainable and financially affordable.

As a Rococo emblem and 'humble' motif that immediately evoked an entire style, the shell also appeared, along with silver-paper stars and pink muslin, in interiors by Stephen Tennant, a notoriously tenuous and eccentric writer, as well as in the home of the no less unusual millionaire and tenuous poet, Edward James. The latter, despite everything, became one of the great patrons of Surrealism and lived in surroundings that reflected the fact.

The shell is also a vital motif in Angus McBean's papier-mâché settings with their Neptunes with cotton-wool beards and spangled mermaids, as well as for Cecil Beaton. Another facet emerges in these examples of English 'good bad taste': the shell has links to theatrical dreams of the seaside, with its sparse vegetation, forlorn beach-huts and endless horizons – improbable spaces, steeped in mystery and opening on to the unknown.

The motif is pictorially inexhaustible: it is to be found as much in the meticulous *trompe-l'oeil* of a Pierre Roy or a Meredith Frampton as in the lyrical melancholy of the Neo-Romantics (Christian Bérard, Léonor Fini, Léonid Berman and others). With Eugène Berman, and his brother Léonid in particular, the crowded shores become the stage for a magnificent decay, a Baroque in tatters, in which shreds of drapery, scraps of wood, pallid plants and polished shells become the materials for an opera of ruin, with *trompe-l'oeil* boards and imaginary scenery.

The same fantasy, the same desire to transform the natural, yet 'humble', marvel of the shell into the most splendid of all objects is to be found in the 1940s in Fulco di Verdura. Verdura, a Sicilian aristocrat accustomed to seeing the extremes of poverty and wealth existing side by side, began by designing costume jewelry for Chanel (who then claimed to have discovered him) before opening his own business in the United States. He is credited with sublime *objets trouvés*, in which a simple scallop shell, or some other sea creature, is overlaid with a whole constellation of rubies or emeralds to create a unique, and utterly incongruous, gem.

At the same time, Jean Schlumberger, using more orthodox materials but in a vocabulary that always reflected, or rather re-created, Rocaille forms, had eyes only for the shell, of which he left some truly startling interpretations.

These two goldsmiths, Verdura and Schlumberger, find their match as creators of '*fantaisie*' in a virtuoso self-taught artist whose significance has still to be properly recognized. She will undoubtedly last as one of the most productive personalities of the 'forties' style. Line Vautrin, producing limited editions of objects and jewels in gilded bronze, and later in resin, has devised pieces of rare inventiveness and boundless ingenuity that come half-way between traditional costume jewelry and the precious creations of the goldsmith. The shell gave her one of her simplest and finest motifs (*Ammonite* of about 1949), as well as the material for a series of covered boxes in engraved mother-of-pearl.

This range of examples shows the shell's significance in the decorative arts from the 1930s to the 1950s. It provided a key motif by linking the purest geometry and the strongest plastic qualities to the poetry of the elements and to metaphors of the shore and of wide open spaces. It was also the recurring dream of an epoch – the Rocaille – symbolizing the whole carefree, splendid and improbable eighteenth century. Finally, it provided a key motif in its 'humbleness', which made it all the better suited to an assertion of extreme sophistication and lent itself to treatment in a precarious, and for that reason all the more highly prized, material: plaster. The preference of the age for plaster was not, as might be thought, merely a reflection of economic pressures: its use by Jean-Michel Frank, Diego Giacometti and Serge Roche preceded the war years and the consequent shortages and necessary recourse to less costly materials. It was rather the very texture of this substance, its fragile solidity, the powdery dullness of its surface, the subtlety of its tones, the way in which it refracted light, and, not least, its complete contrast to the accepted 'noble' materials such as marble and bronze; in a word, it was the very aesthetic quality of the plaster object that the creative artists of the half-century sought to exploit to its fullest.

Epochs speak through their taste for materials that first please, then bore, go out of fashion and finally disappear. Plaster, fallen from use since the 1950s, reappeared in the language of contemporary creative artists after a gap of thirty years. It is one index of a revolution in taste. The various connoisseurs, collectors and artists (never to the fore but influential behind the scenes) who had responded too hastily to the debasement of Modernism soon disappeared from the official histories and the calendar of taste, surviving only in faint traces of their influence. It had to fall to the new generations, born in mid-century and with only a muddled understanding of those ways, forms and styles, to do justice to all these anomalies and to resuscitate the lost motifs.

As if in a Chinese fable, we dream today of the Rococo that was admired and transformed by Edith Sitwell, Cyril Connolly or Carlos de Beistegui. A shell hat by Christian Lacroix or by Krizia is an echo of an echo; their starting point is a drawing by Beaton or a detail by Schiaparelli, which themselves are the product of a dazzling feature of Sanssouci, or of an arabesque by Pillement or Lajoue. Similarly, the fantastic objects by Thomas Boog or Leïla Menchari's décors for Hermès are a borrowing from the meticulous settings of A la Ronde, from the end of the eighteenth century as revisited by *Regency Vogue* of the 1940s and adapted to new uses.... The shell may become, as it was for Jean-Charles Moreux in 1951, a subject for contemplation, an object in a new cabinet of curiosities. It is at once contradictory and familiar, magical and banal, steeped in history and absolutely natural, the marvel of a theatre with many backcloths, or split screens, opening on illusionist infinities; and somehow all the more fascinating for that.

Born in Nantes, Brittany, in 1880, Pierre Roy cultivated a personal kind of Surrealism all his life, whose formal mastery has certain affinities with the work of Meredith Frampton in England. His paintings consist for the most part of impossible still-lifes in the form of architectures of objects that have a very similar atmosphere to those of De Chirico. He exhibited for the first time in France in 1928 and in New York two years later. Possessing a private fortune, he was able to work simply as he pleased, became 'the most accomplished accredited Surrealist contributor' to American Vogue, and painted in all no more than 275 pictures in his whole life. He died in Milan in 1950. Pierre Roy frequently returned to the dreamy theme of the sea-shore, and shells, in pictures with a colouring that ranges from the coldest and most sombre hues to the glossy pinks and blues of these two works: **Pink Bow and Shell beside the Sea**, undated, and **Still Life, 1947.**

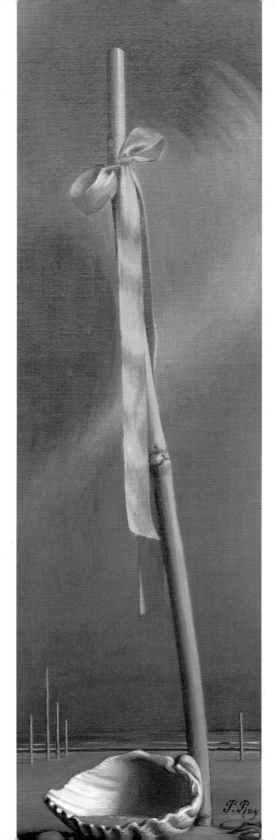

Painter, illustrator and theatrical designer, Eugène Berman (1899–1972), along with his brother Léonid, Christian Bérard and Pavel Tchelitchew, belonged to the Neo-Romantic group that was formed in Paris in the early 1930s. Incomparable as a draughtsman, Berman created a dreamlike, desolate world influenced by Roman Baroque and

*the colours of Italy. He is the supreme representative of the easy erudition, playful sophistication and allusive fantasy that 'reinvented' the shell theme in the thirties, such as the collage on paper of a woman's head with shell motifs (**opposite**), and the profile of a woman on a pebble with shells attached, set against a velvet background in a stained-glass frame (**left**).*

Lover of curiosities, creator of objects and specialist in the history of frames and mirrors (on which he compiled two imposing volumes), Serge Roche was one of the misunderstood stylists of the first half of the present century who rediscovered the spirit of the Rocaille and of the eighteenth century. He worked with Jean-Michel Frank and was very close in spirit to the designs of Syrie Maugham in England.

Left: *Three wooden shells limewashed a creamy white, 1940s (the two larger measuring 20 x 25 cm, the smaller 20 x 12 cm).*

Opposite, above left: *Plaster wall-light by Serge Roche (45 x 30 cm), c. 1930. There was also a ceiling light in a variation of the theme.*

Opposite, below: *Plaster lamp base by Diego and Alberto Giacometti for Jean-Michel Frank, 1930s.*

Opposite, above right: *Jean-Charles Moreux, terracotta vase with antique green patina, 1940 (40 x 30 cm). The nautilus was one of the key forms in Moreux's world. He reinterpreted it in many ways, even using it in its fossil form* (see page 108).

In the thirties and forties, Fulco di Verdura revived a whole Baroque catalogue of dolphins, unicorns, blackamoors, putti and shells, while giving them a completely new interpretation. He made much play with the contrasts between 'noble' and 'humble' materials, enriching shells with gold and precious stones. Above right: *Scallop encrusted with yellow gold, diamonds and sapphires, 1939.*

The unpretentious ornamentalist Line

Vautrin, working with gilt bronze and resin in small series, used the shell and fossil theme in powder compacts, ashtrays and pin-trays. **Below left:**

Ammonite, *gilt bronze, 1940s.*

In 1936, René Boivin spangled the spirals of a shell brooch with precious stones (**below centre**), while Jean Schlumberger, master of fantasy, frequently returned to the shell theme with an inventiveness that was always fresh. Opposite: *Jewel design by Schlumberger for Pauline de Rothschild, 1940s.*

For the gallery owner Naïla de Monbrison in 1993, Marcial Berro took up again the idea of combining plain and precious materials in this shell brooch (**below right**) embellished with silver, gold and grey pearls.

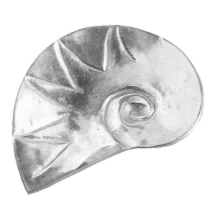

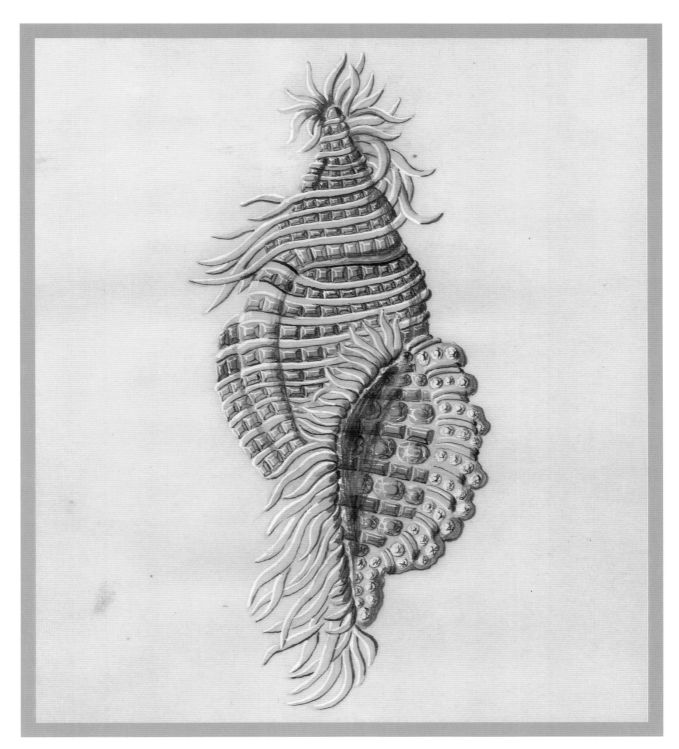

The shell belongs naturally to the realm of Venice and the sea, providing in particular an inexhaustible motif for the Venetian glasshouses.

Left: *Ashtray or pin-tray in the form of a conch shell, with gold iridescence and milky body-paste, Veltrarti, Venice, 1940s.*

Below left: *Glass shell worked with acid, Véronèse, Paris, 1940.*

Below: *Four shells in iridescent glass with gold inclusions, Véronèse, Paris, 1940.*

Opposite: *Important blown-glass shell with gold inclusions, Alfredo Barbini, Venice, c. 1945 (20 x 40 cm).*

Linked in the immediate post-war years with artists such as Eugène Berman, Max Ernst and Léonor Fini, Piero Fornasetti (1913–1988), a highly versatile individual whose activities ranged from typography to furniture design, frequently used the shell theme in his products, whether it be on tables, boxes or glassware, or in the 1954 series of plates, Océanidi.

Opposite: *Piero Fornasetti, plate from the series* **Theme and Variations.**

In 1950 Christian Dior produced this set of six hand-painted plates (above) *on which various shells are represented, including nautilus, conch and scallop.*

Busts of bamboo, slate and shells, made by France Sagliot, probably for fashion show-cases, French, c. 1950. Window-dressing and showroom displays in the years following the Second World War underwent a truly extraordinary transformation under the influence of a new-found sophistication, most famously exemplified by Christian Dior. This led to the rediscovery of the art of Janine Janet, for example, whose displays form veritable sculptures. It is this same tradition that Leïla Menchari, perhaps the last of the line, continues to pursue for Hermès.

Founded in 1837, and one of those rare firms that still belong to the family of the original owners, retaining a direct link with the 'shop' that became established before the end of the nineteenth century, Hermès is the very epitome of luxury, the last word in perfection for manufactured objects. The display of this sublime merchandise has always been of paramount importance. The show-windows of Hermès were part of that 'great poem of window-dressing' that Balzac evoked and which so enthused Walter Benjamin. Revived in the immediate post-war years by Annie Baumel as a way of compensating for the shortage of goods, with the help of artists such as Lila de Nobili, Jean Cocteau and Léonor Fini, the displays have for some fifteen years past been the work of Leïla Menchari. Season after season she masterminds a sumptuous stage-set of the ephemeral, with each year being dedicated to a particular theme. Two displays for 1992 are shown here: 'the golden surf' for Christmas (opposite) and 'the crystal grotto' (left), one of the series of 'imaginary grottoes', as well as a window for summer 1984, 'the mother-of-pearl fountain' (above left), which immediately suggests Roman Baroque and the extravagance of Borromini.

In the 1950s Jean-Charles Moreux was among the first to take a new interest in the theme of the shell, the curiosity and the intermixing of artificialia and naturalia. He formed a cabinet of curiosities, designed a set of furniture around the motif of the shell, and wrote an unpublished paper on the subject – the inspiration, in part, for the present book. It is logical therefore to draw towards the end with these candlesticks by Moreux based on a pair of fossilized nautilus shells.

In pursuit of his totally original work, Thomas Boog succeeded in 'reinventing' the mid-nineteenth-century tradition of shellwork objects. These dreamlike pieces – frames, mirrors and candlesticks combining shells and coral – have a strikingly magical aura.

Opposite: *Large frame encrusted with shells in a harmony of mother-of-pearl and chestnut colour (160 x 130 cm).* **Inset:** *Five-branched candelabrum with iridescent shells and sprigs of red coral (80 cm high); wooden ball covered with* Umbonium costanum *shells (diameter 20 cm).*

REFERENCES

Foreword

Wheeler, Mortimer, 'A Symbol in Ancient Times' in Ian Cox (ed.), *The Scallop. Studies of a Shell and its Influences on Humankind*, 'Shell' Transport and Trading Company, Limited, London, 1957, pp. 33-48

Hohler, Christopher, 'The Badge of St James' in *The Scallop, op. cit.*, pp. 49-72

Chapter One **The Shapely Shell**

Valéry, Paul, 'L'Homme et la Coquille', in *Variété*, vol. 1, Gallimard, Paris, 1957, pp. 886-907

Moreux, Jean-Charles, 'Coquilles', typescript, Fonds Jean-Charles Moreux, Institut Français d'Architecture, Paris, 1947

Chapter Two **The Curio Cabinet**

Schlosser, J. von, *Die Kunst- und Wunderkammern der Spätrenaissance*, Klinkhardt & Biermann, Leipzig, 1908 (or Italian translation by P. Di Paolo, *Raccolte d'arte e di meraviglie del tardo Rinascimento*, Sansoni, Florence, 1974, pp. 9-25)

Coomans, Henry, 'Conchology before Linnaeus', in Oliver Impey and Arthur MacGregor (eds), *The Origins of Museums*, Clarendon Press, Oxford, 1985, pp. 188-94

MacGregor, Arthur (ed.), *Tradescant's Rarities*, Clarendon Press, Oxford, 1983

Lugli, Adalgisa, *Naturalia et mirabilia*, G. Mazotta, Milan, [1983]

Schnapper, Antoine, *Le Géant, la licorne et la tulipe*, Flammarion, Paris, 1988, pp. 71-74

Chapter Three **The Mannerist Shell**

Jones, Barbara, *Follies and Grottoes*, 2nd edn, Constable, London, 1974, p. 148

Zehnacker, Françoise, and Petit, Nicolas, *Le Cabinet de curiosités de la Bibliothèque Sainte-Geneviève*, exhibition catalogue, Paris, 1989, p. 101

Berti, Luciano, *Il principe dello studiolo. Francesco I dei Medici e la fine del Rinascimento fiorentino*, EDAM, Florence, 1967, pp. 61-84

Soscino, A.S., *Cabinet d'amateur, le grandi collezioni d'arte nei dipinti dal XVII al XIX secolo*, Berenice, Milan, 1992, pp. 31ff.

Chapter Four **The Rocaille Flourish**

Gruber, Alain Charles (ed.), and Pons, Bruno, *L'Art décoratif en Europe: Classique et Baroque*, Citadelles & Mazenod, Paris, 1992, p. 333

Kimball, Fiske Sidney, *The Creation of the Rococo*, Philadelphia Museum of Art, Philadelphia, 1943, p. 160

Connolly, Cyril, *Previous Convictions*, Hamish Hamilton, London, 1963, pp. 48-50

Evans, Joan, *Pattern*, vol. 2, Clarendon Press, Oxford, 1931, pp. 90-94

Chapter Five **Fantastic Architecture**

Battisti, Eugenio, *L'antirinascimento*, 2nd edn, vol. 1, Garzanti, Milan, 1989, pp. 204-14

Luchinat, Cristina Acidini, and Magnani, Lauro (eds), *Arte delle grotte*, conference proceedings, 17 June 1985, SAGEP, Genoa, 1987, p. 43ff.

Cameron, Roderick, 'Formes naturelles' in *L'Oeil*, 38, February 1958, Paris, Lausanne: A. Zwemmer, London, pp. 45-57

La Fontaine, Jean de, 'Les amours de Psyché' in *Oeuvres complètes*, vol. 2, Gallimard, Paris, 1943, pp. 130-32

Villemin, V., and Langlois, G.A., *Les sept folies capitales*, Editions Alternatives, Paris, 1986, pp. 69-86

Lawson Dick, Oliver (ed.), *Aubrey's Brief Lives*, Penguin Books, Harmondsworth, 1972, pp. 202-5

Jones, Barbara, *Follies and Grottoes, op. cit.*, pp. 149 and 156

Day, Angelique (ed.), *Letters from Georgian Ireland: The Correspondence of Mary Delany, 1731-1768*, Friar's Bush Press, Belfast, 1992, pp. 246-47

Jones, Barbara, *Follies and Grottoes, op. cit.*, pp. 157-59

Cook, Olive, and Smith, Edwin, 'Beside the Seaside' in John Hadfield (ed.), *The Saturday Book*, vol. 12, Hutchinson, London, 1952, pp. 22-44 (in p. 43)

Chapter Six **Kitsch and Grotto Furniture**

Evans, Joan, *Pattern, op. cit.*, p. 89

Laver, James, 'The Cradle of Venus' in *The Scallop, op. cit.*, pp. 87-88

Newman, Bruce, and Duncan, Alastair, *Fantasy Furniture*, Rizzoli, New York, 1989, pp. 60-64)

Chapter Seven **The Baroque Dream**

Day, Susan, *Louis Süe: architectures*, Pierre Mardaga, Liège, 1986, pp. 59-60

Battersby, Martin, *The Decorative Thirties*, rev. and ed. by Philippe Garner, Herbert Press, London, 1988, pp. 176-77 and 188

The Contents of Wilsford Manor, Wiltshire, sale catalogue, Sotheby's, London, October 1987

The Edward James Collection, sale catalogue, Christie's, London, June 1986

Soby, James Thrall, *After Picasso*, Edwin Valentine Mitchell, Hartford, and Dodd Mead & Co., New York, 1935, pp. 11-56

d'Ormesson, Jean, and Vreeland, Diana, *Jean Schlumberger*, Franco Maria Ricci, Milan, 1976, pp. 69-111

Vautrin, Line, and Mauriès, Patrick, *Line Vautrin: Jeweller, Sculptor, Magician*, Thames and Hudson, London and New York, 1992

Martin, Richard, *Fashion and Surrealism*, Thames and Hudson, London, and Rizzoli, New York, 1990, pp. 148-56

Moreux, Jean-Charles, 'Coquilles', *op. cit.*

INDEX

PHOTO CREDITS AND ACKNOWLEDGMENTS

Hubert Josse 1, 2/3, 4, 5, 6, 7, 8, 12, 43, 44, 45, 46, 47, 58, 59, 60, 61, 62, 63, 64, 65, 77, 78, 79, 81, 82, 83, 84, 85, 94, 95, 96, 97, 98 *below*, 100, 101, 103, 104, 105, 108, 109.

All rights reserved 94; Marcial Berro 98 *below right*; Andrew Bettles 9; courtesy CRC 60 *above*; Christie's Images 33; Copenhagen, Det Danske Kunstindustrimuseet 49; Richard L. Feigen and Company, New York (© SPADEM) 92; courtesy Barnaba Fornasetti 102; Hamburg, Kunsthalle 20; A.F. Kersting 70/71; Lucinda Lambton/Arcaid 72, 73; Guillaume de Laubier/Hermès 106, 107; By courtesy of the Trustees, The

National Gallery, London 31; Georgina Masson 68 *below*, 69 *left*; Musée de Neuilly-sur-Seine, Centre Culturel Arturo Lopez 6; Bruce M. Newman, *Fantasy Furniture*, Rizzoli International Publications Inc. 80 *below*; Paris: L'Arc-en-Seine (© ADAGP) 96 *below*, Musée des Arts Décoratifs 46, Bibliothèque Nationale 60 *below*, Thomas Boog 109, Les Couleurs du Temps, collection Jean-Pierre Chalon 104, 105, Stéphane Deschamps 2, 3, 96 *above left*, Epoca 7, 12, 79 *below left*, 81, 83, Patrick Fourtin 108, Yves Gastou 5, 96 *above right*, 97, 98 *below centre*, 100, 101, 103, l'Imprévu 79 *above left* and *above and below right*, 84,

85, Musée du Louvre 1, 30 (© Photo RMN), 47, Galerie du Passage (all rights reserved) 95, Galerie André-François Petit (© SPADEM) 93, Musée du Petit-Palais 44, 45; Private Collection 14, 83; Domaine National de Rambouillet 64, 65; Scala 26, 27; Sèvres, Musée National de Céramique 82; Edwin Smith 66, 67, 69 *right*, courtesy Verdura, New York 98 *above*; Vienna, Kunsthistorisches Museum 21.

The author and publisher would like to thank the following for the kind assistance they provided during the preparation of this book:

M. Marcial Berro, M. Thomas Boog, M. Boutonnet, Mme Marie-France Boyer, M. Jean-Pierre Chalon, Galerie Les Couleurs du Temps, CRC, M. Stéphane Deschamps, L'Etude Binoche et Godeaut, M. Patrick Fourtin, M. Yves Gastou, M. François Giroux, Mme Martine Jeannin, M. Hubert Josse, M. Christian Lacroix, M. Pierre Le-Tan, Mme Mona Linz-Einstein, Mme Leïla Menchari, Mme Monique Mosser, Mme Françoise de Nobèle, M. Pierre Passebon, M. Jean Rosen, M. Nicolas Sarkozy, Mme Setton, Mme Pascale Siegrist, M. Jean-Michel Smilenko, Mme Line Vautrin.